ETCHED FOREVER

RHYTHMIC PUBLISHERS

Made with ♥ on the Notion Press Platform
www.notionpress.com

Contents

Rhythmic Publishers

-Seeking harmony through words

We, at *Rhythmic Publishers,* believe in the power of words as a means of seeking harmony in a chaotic universe. We are eager to provide aspiring writers with a premium platform to express themselves. Attractive packages are available for both solo books and anthologies (editorial services and book design included). We work diligently to make a book the best version of itself and client satisfaction is our top priority.

Contact us on:
Instagram: @rhythmicpublishers
E-mail: rhythmicpublications23@gmail.com
We are also on **Twitter** and **LinkedIn**

Disclaimer

This anthology is a collection of poems, stories and write-ups written by talented writers from various parts of the country.

We have guided them not to use any copyrighted content and done our best to check plagiarism.

If any copyrighted content is detected, neither the publisher, nor the compiler nor the editor will be responsible in any way. Co-authors will be responsible for their own content.

Compiler and Editor: Aishi Bandyopadhyay

Book Layout and Cover Design: Romit Majumder

Acknowledgements

***Rhythmic Publishers** expresses its gratitude towards the extremely talented co-authors, who have enthusiastically contributed their write-ups for this book.*

About The Book

Etched Forever is an anthology that takes the readers on a trip down memory lane. The essays and poems included within the folds of this book paint a picture of a time that's gone by. Some of them are introspective and trace the evolution of the past self into the present self. The book is a testimony to the indubitable role of memories in shaping the human existence. It is indeed a collection of moments and reminiscences that leave a lasting impact on the heart.

1

Whispers from the Past...

Dr Sukanya Bhattacharya

Through life's journey, I trudge along.
Shades of multiple hues colour my path
What remain are mere shadows of the past
Looming large silhouettes of the past.
Some fond memories of loved ones indelibly etched in my heart.
The rest, best to be forgotten, but alas!
They act as peeping Tommies, making their presence felt at unexpected gloomy moments, causing much distress.
At times, I burst into full throated laughter, and gladness fills my soul, as I recount the silly jokes I had shared with friends not too long ago.
What seems like aeons ago is just a few moons back.
I take recourse to all these joys I had shared in yesteryears.
My pet dog, Lassy, now across the rainbow bridge, my best companion gone too soon...

He would trot beside me, his legs walking overtime, his leash would bounce to the rhythm of his snorts, savouring every small moment that life offered.

So many deaths, too much to bear, I do not know how to process both Sorrow and Joy.

Still, the lasting imprints left of them, leave a deep ache of losing all too soon.

Thus, I am sharing a life cratered with imperfections, a life yet to be lived, loved and enjoyed till I make my transition to the other side.

2

Luminous Serene Childhood

Deyasini Roy

The minute you put a full stop on a particular work, the next moment it becomes a memory. Isn't it amazing? Yes, it is indeed. Strolling meticulously through my life till date, I find it surreal that I have built tons of memories to share: some good, some horrendous, some ludicrous, some highly appreciative and emotional.

The most cherished moments of my life that will remain etched forever in my heart are my innocent days of childhood: a time when a four-year-old me, wearing a quintessential white *Tep Jama* (a small white frock with kantha stitch work), dancing to the tunes of Rabindra Sangeet playing on the tape recorder, was actually weaving together sumptuous amounts of love, warmth and serenity. Back then, birthdays did not mean a mandatory 12 o' clock wish and writing grand wishes on WhatsApp, but rather, multiple rings of the landline. The automated telephone statement, “The number you have dialed is busy,” would truly prove how important and loved one would feel on birthdays. The *rannar thakur* (cook) would be allotted a place in the house and the grandeur smell of Pulao, Soft Juicy *Kosha* Mutton coming from there would make me ecstatic. The simple “*Chandaner* Design” beautifully painted on the forehead during birthdays, was surely a joyous moment.

The unanimous melodious ringing of Nokia cell phones is yet another piece of time from my childhood that I miss terribly. The happiness of welcoming the first communicative device in a family was indeed a big deal back then. The snake game in it was addictive and it was a real challenge to complete all the levels. The mobile, tied as a locket for the elderly, was an interesting fashion of that time.

Transportation traverses people to new, unexplored and unexpected destinations. The body and the mind for a minute retrogrades. Sounding like a riddle? Confused? Don’t be! I am talking about my childhood days of travelling by tram, bus, red-and-yellow-coloured autos, the black and white coloured taxis. I loved travelling on the tram. Although it was slow, it had a mesmerizing charm. Now, when I ponder, I feel that it gave me the chance to taste the history of the 19th century, to patiently absorb the changes in landscape and commuters, and last but not the least, to enjoy the ringing of the bell.

The mini private buses with wooden panels and seats, two-door facilities to get inside, and also a rare ticket checker, who might jump in at any point, truly characterized the interior of an early 2000's bus. The hustle and bustle, the severe pushing, standing on the last step of the bus and compelled pulling of the rope to put it to halt at the required places were all quintessential to the stormy attitude of the buses.

The earliest picture of autos flashing in my mind shows a black hood covering them. The gradual transition, from full ghostly black to green and yellow, indicates the emergence of LPG-run autos. When I remember the excitement of riding in it, it makes me recall how little things in life would matter a lot back then. Sitting inside a new auto for a hearty ride was something I would look forward to then, and still do now.

The underground metro is another such transport which highly fascinates me and has formed endless memories in my life till date. Earlier, those yellow ochre movable structures, without air conditioners and glass-shut rectangle-shaped windows with railings, resonated that life was much simpler. Kolkata, although being a metropolitan city, was not following in the footsteps of other cities and countries in trying to renovate the styling of the trains. As time has passed, my inner soul has made me realize, that the little chirpy me, who was bound to travel in the crowd, would eventually skip one or two rides, just to travel at ease, escaping from the indomitable heat and enjoying the blissful ride of a newly installed air conditioner, taking a step closer to the luxuries of life. Little did I know that those were the golden days of my life which can never be forgotten. A metro ride was, and still is, a positive one, because it resonates the feeling that there is light at the end of the tunnel. One must not stop taking their righteous, brave strides in life.

How can transportation draw back memories which will remain forever in our hearts?

Well, it does, because every day, apart from our families, those that regularly notice the changes in our lives are these vehicles, right from the beginning of our childhood, when we first learned to walk. The first probable vehicles that we used were the perambulators which made us create a connection with the outer world and took us to places like the parks, the neighbourhood, to the relatives' houses and to other special occasions.

The first independent bus or tram ride from school or tuitions with friends was always special. Leading a sheltered life during schooldays, my first solo travel on a bus from school to my maternal grandparents' house was a treat to the soul. There were butterflies in my stomach as the bus journey proceeded. It made me feel the first taste of freedom, much like a bird that flies for the first time from its nest.

The rush to take the window seat in the carpool and to sadly tolerate the buzzing commuters inside the carpool bus, immaculately explaining the four 'Wives' (what, when, where, why) and one 'Husband' (how) of any serious incident that occurred at any time of that day, also comes to mind. The 'bus', at that moment, was our abode to donate our footages of tenure at school.

Providing a mandatory routinized update to my mother,

after school, was of sheer joy to me. Like a garrulous speaker, I would make her listen to my speech, with no answer from the other side, which would make me angry. The only response that I would receive is, "I will listen to you whole-heartedly at night. Hang up the call and freshen up now.'

Such adorable, sweet, beautiful pictures come to my mind whenever I fall back upon the past. This is what keeps me going at the end of the day.

The smallest of the small events in our lives is what we call memories. When a string of the kite gets detached from it, you are unable to make it fly. Similarly, memories, unless formed, cannot help you to lead your life. Dreams are meant to be broken, it is said, but, memories are not. Once formed, they stay forever and ever.

3

A Maiden of Ind

Monoswita Biswas

Her eyes laden with *kajal*
Bejewelled there she stands
The parting of her head
With red vermillion smeared
On someone's request
To be Isabella she dares
Thinks she what woe her fate shall bring
Thick long hair she has
Doe eyed maiden is she
Her feet painted with red lilac
Conch shells on her hand she bears
Maid of Ind is she
Her every heartbeat bears her country's glory
European in thought she may be.

To be Isabella
Alack! What misfortune lies ahead!
If she were Isabella
Edward her lord, her husband dear.
To be faithful to him
She swore before God
But! Alas!
Her husband in love with his minion dear
Lonely maiden eagerly waits
The larks screech
Comes the dawn once again
No *Savitri* or *Behula* is she

The Dusk falls
Flickers off the light
Apollo plays the sweetest music all night long
Sing all the cherubs
Tonight it's so sweet
Smells the garden of jasmine
Ah! So sweet the smell!
In trance the maiden knows not where she is
Such earthly pleasures!
Does a maiden deserve?

Ah! Edward I pity thee
Bear no wrath
A flower was dying of draught
To water the dried plant
What sin had Mortimer done?
Watered the plant,
Nursed it back in your presence.

Oh! Edward
Do be kind!
The garden may be yours,
But, whoever eyes these flowers
And plucks them
They belong to him hence.

4

Didama and Hanuman

Dr. Debasri Mukherjee

I was floating in that magical place between sleep and wakefulness, lulled by the soft sigh of the waves. The eternal river Ganga flowed on her endless path forever and ever. The dulcet tones of a conversation pulled me back from the land of dreams. Someone was talking. I half opened my eyes, expecting to see my parents conversing with my grandmother, but the room was empty! I sat up to look at the door. It was locked from the inside. Then where was my grandmother?

I got off the bed and wrapped myself in a warm blanket. Even though it was the end of April, it was chilly in Rishikesh, where we were currently visiting. Plus, our hotel was right on the banks of the river, making it especially cold in the early mornings and late evenings. I was shivering despite the blanket.

I glanced around the room. The washroom door was ajar.

So, my grandmother wasn't in the washroom either. That was when I heard her voice again, apparently coming from the balcony. What was she doing out in the balcony this early? And who was she talking to? Agog with curiosity, I stepped out onto the balcony and stopped dead with shock. It must be a monkey, I assumed, since it had a tail, but in all other aspects, it was akin to a gorilla. It was huge! Its head was almost touching the lintel as it sat on the balcony rail. Its tail was at least three feet long and hanging down to the balcony below us. It was a bright golden-grey, the color of sunlight reflecting off old hay, and had a black face with widespread black/brown eyes that were regarding me with open curiosity. Mine, on the other hand, were round with shock and fear.

My grandmother's cheerful voice snapped me back to my senses. I turned my head slightly, keeping the mythological specimen in my peripheral vision, to look at my grandmother. She was sitting on one of the chairs and was still in her night clothes. I noticed that she had a packet of biscuits in her hand. After some time, I became aware of what she was saying. "This is Hanuman, darling. He has come to visit us and is asking how we like his town. Won't you come here and talk to him?" I stared at my grandmother like she had lost her mind. She was a frail woman of seventy years. The mythological monkey could rip her head off in one try if it wanted to. But, at the moment, it didn't seem to be in the mood. In fact, it was now staring at my grandmother in rapturous adoration like she was the savior he had dreamed about (I assumed it was a he, although I didn't have any categorical evidence supporting the assumption).

My earliest memories of my maternal grandmother were the smell of coral jasmine (shiuli) and animals. She had birds, cats and dogs. Animals automatically knew that my grandmother was a kindred spirit. The shyest of creatures would trust her to take care of them. I used to accompany her on her many missions of mercy, climbing trees to rescue baby pigeons or crawling through cubby holes to extract a litter of kittens. So, it was but natural that she would call me to her side on this new adventure. However, baby birds, kittens, and puppies were one thing, but this magnificent specimen of Semnopithecus was a completely different story. However, my grandmother's charm seemed to have worked on him too. He was now politely accepting another biscuit from her hand and listening attentively as she introduced me. I tentatively made my way to her side and for the first time looked the monkey directly in the eyes. They were kind and wise, without even a hint of aggression. He seemed ancient, and seemed to comprehend everything my grandmother was saying. I smiled at him and was sure that I saw the corners of his eyes crinkle in answer to that. I turned my head to look at my grandmother. She was already looking at me, and a spark of shared knowledge passed between us. We were kindred spirits.

The jarring notes of the doorbell startled us out of our reverie. We both turned towards the door. When we turned back, Hanuman was gone without a trace. We stared for a few moments at the empty space where he was sitting a few seconds ago. Now all that remained was the memory and the empty biscuit packet in my grandmother's hand. We let out a collective sigh and walked together to open the door.

5

A Journey to "SELF"

Sanchita Chakraborty

Water has always been a source of fear for me—the exquisite depth, the stark white foam that dances upon its surface, the breathless sensation it creates as it engulfs everything in its embrace—all of it evokes a sense of awe and fear in my mind. I used to think that the vastness of water would take me away from myself; I feared I would be lost forever in this unending battle against the unknown forces of nature. But, nature had other plans for me.

As the youngest girl in a large joint family, I felt like a small stream lost in a mighty river. My family's love and expectations were like strong currents, carrying me wherever they flowed. Being the only girl in a sea of brothers made me feel like the sparkling surface of water, reflecting everyone's dream. But, as I moved with the current, I forgot about my own source – the quiet spring inside me that wanted to flow in its own direction.

Fortunately, as the years passed, time introduced me to a few enlightening souls who helped me grasp the profound importance of self-discovery. Initially, I perceived them as somewhat selfish, questioning how one could even prioritize oneself above the familial bonds we share. However, I began to understand that I am a separate entity, and others, while important, hold a secondary place in the hierarchy of my existence. This idea hit me like a bolt of lightning.

For quite some time, melancholy became my constant companion, lurking at the edges of my happiness. However, everything shifted when I made a sudden visit to the serene River. The long river, the clear blue water, the towering trees, and the tranquil island prompted deep introspection. I unearthed a 'new me' that words often fail to capture. I realized that a moment of solitude is not just beneficial, but essential. The silence that enveloped me, the gentle sound of crickets chirping in the backdrop, and the soothing breeze that once evoked a sense of melancholy, began to transform into the pleasure I had sought for so long.

On that enlightening day, I realized that a solitary moment of contemplation—often misinterpreted as sadness—could serve as a powerful catalyst for clarifying one's understanding of self. The version of myself that was perpetually surrounded by a happy family, merely moving through life and embodying adjustment, was not the embodiment of true living. Instead, I recognized that I had become akin to the character "Dory", endlessly seeking the approval of others while losing my own identity in the process. I pondered over the question: is it genuinely possible to fulfil everyone's dreams while remaining completely unaware of my own self?

Through the stillness of the deep water, the green surroundings, the tranquil nature, the blue sky, the warm sun, and the sweet, earthy scent filling the air, I started to grasp the essential difference between selfless love and the sacrifices of personal identity. While my current way of living was satisfactory, I realized that establishing boundaries was not just desirable, but necessary. Leading a happy life within the warmth of a happy family is indeed crucial, but, I could no longer overlook the vital practices of self-talk and meditation. I learned that while it's important for "Doraemon" to always come up with innovative solutions for Nobita, it's equally important for him to take out time for himself, sit under a cherry blossom tree and enjoy dorayaki. It's not wrong to be caring and generous towards others, but, there must always be room for taking care of oneself, if not as a top priority, then at least as a consideration that is not to be ignored.

I discovered that my deepest fear was not the unknown depths of the water; rather, it was succumbing to the weight of others' expectations, ultimately losing the essence of who I truly am. I realized that the silence which had once spurred melancholy now whispered back profound truths that the crowd could never convey.

Embracing moments of solitude does not equate to loneliness; it is instead a powerful reclamation of self and identity. My all-consuming fear—once paralyzing—has ultimately guided me towards clarity and strength. The stillness of the water, the gentle rustling of the trees in the soft wind, and the warmth of the sun on my skin, collectively reminded me that life itself is about seeking balance. It's about the delicate art of giving to others, yet also pausing just long enough to receive. I understood, deeply, that in order to be truly present for those I care about, I must first be wholeheartedly present for myself.

This newfound realization is not an ending, but rather, a beginning, and so, my journey continues...

PPP

6

The Sixth Decade

Dr Sukanya Bhattacharya

Creaky knees, frozen shoulders, knocked out joints and
a shock of grey hair.
The mirror that once portrayed your young, vibrant,
vivacious self now reveals a woman totally transformed.
The metamorphosis is unbelievable but the mirror does
not lie. How I wish I could morph back to my old self.
The clock cannot unwind, it ticks away...
You have always said that age is just a number but the
number does impact you in numerous ways.
The crow's feet, age spots, fine lines and wrinkles, a
lacklustre rugged skin has replaced the silky soft creamy
texture that your skin had once been.
You wonder: Is this really me? You shudder and shy
away, denial occupies your mindscape.
The dainty, slender physique that once was yours could
never be the couch potato's you've turned out to be.
Your knees hurt as you climb the flight of stairs. Your
teeth ache when you brush.

You realize that you are no longer that log of wood that slept for hours. Just a few hours now keeps you going.

You watch in dismay, your lipid levels spike, BP reaches a high. You are put on meds and grossly afraid to indulge in sweet delights.

You take a bite, your cravings amplify. Chocolate is just too good to let go of.

A slice of choco brownie throws you off the trajectory.

You wince in pain as your stomach refuses to budge.

The sinful indulgence is no longer meant for you.

Your bottle of antacid is now your friend in need, not the can of Pepsi that you savoured in the past.

The lip-smacking fast food, a sure recipe for disaster.

On the doctor's advice you keep a step away.

You satiate your taste buds with your usual cup of coffee, fruits, salads and greens. You struggle to raise your endorphins, slowly, cautiously.

The only icing on the cake is your dwindling but committed friends galore, who not only laugh together, but also stay together.

They say walking helps relieve stress and weight loss too, but, that's a tedious job, won't go overboard for that too.

Going to the gym is just another bane.

I'd better be left alone. I've grown to love my curvy self, so who cares what the scales tell? Am happy with just the way I age.

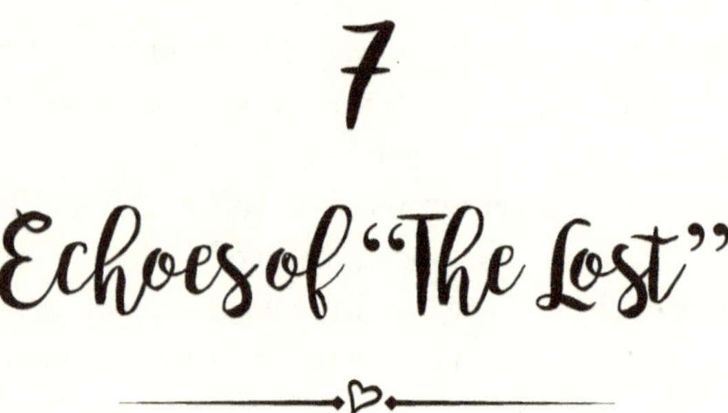

Shreya Ghose

"My tongue will tell the anger of my heart, or else my heart concealing it will break."
— William Shakespeare, The Taming of the Shrew

Dealing with the Departed

Isn't it weird when suddenly you realise they are no more? The helplessness, the slow breathing, the mind fog, and managing emotions simultaneously becomes an overwhelming task. You see them, and you telepathically ask them questions, perhaps to gulp down your own guilt better. Were my actions right? Did I do justice to the eternal bond formed? Once again, there is so much darkness everywhere, and no one to actually feel what you feel.

The flashbacks do no good either; it is like a tingling pain all throughout. How could the two of the closest people now become a distant memory? Why did it have to happen so soon?

I am sure anyone who has lost a loved one has felt this tingling sensation sometime in their life. I call this phase 'complicated grief' — an intense, prolonged, and often debilitating form of grief that can interfere with daily functioning.

The whole point initially involves overplaying your role into every situation, cursing yourself, being in self-doubt, having an unstable mind, and always keeping your guard up. Overall, trying to be extra happy on the outside, but internally battling your own war against yourself. You see, a lot of things I say right now, won't make sense if you read things literally, but would be better decoded if feelings are put in place. After all, it's you, and your feelings against the world.

How would the people around you know the depth of your relationship with the departed? How will they ever understand how much of your life's trajectory immediately hit a major blow, with your loved ones crossing the rainbow bridge?

Then the rational mind suddenly rings the doorbell. It says, isn't death the inevitable truth? Isn't everything temporary? But the heart has decision-making powers too. It won't let rational thinking get the best of our emotions. It will ensure we shed tears, it will ensure we have those sleepless nights, it will ensure we create a new 'I', with every passing day. It's also the most traditional approach to healing. This is how it's done. The hours become days, the months become years, and miraculously the pain seems to take a backstage.

By now, you are out of the complicated grief stage and have stepped into 'emotional paralysis' — a disconnect with one's own feelings. Yes, you function just like your usual self, but there is a sudden change to your personality. You try not to talk about this chapter of your life much, and entertain questions around it, not unless you feel like it. You are now busy playing the role you are set to play in your current phase.

"All the world's a stage,
And all the men and women merely players;
They have their exits and their entrances;
And one man in his time plays many parts,
His acts being seven ages."
— William Shakespeare, As You Like It

About Me

Introducing myself, a 27-year-old Gen Z, considering herself to be part of the millennial community, seeing the likes of Box TVs, my grandmother's antique radio, and my mother's Kotak reel camera. Yes, I am a cusp, self-proclaimed, but it is true.

Being born and brought up in South Kolkata, today, I find myself working at a leading conglomerate in the city. My journey has been shaped by diverse experiences, whether it is Kolkata, Mumbai, or Bangalore, where I have studied and worked previously. I started earning young at a mere age of twenty-two, while pursuing my masters, thanks to Mumbai. I then further broadened horizons to the tech hub Bangalore. The road has been long and winding, but it has been one filled with growth, learning, and a deep commitment to pushing boundaries. And the best part? I have just gotten started.

The First Lost Gem – My Grandmother

This is the story of two very essential assets of my life, due to whom I am the woman I am today: My grandmother, Smt. Manasi Ghose, and my pet dog, Mishti.

Let's start with my grandmother.

My grandmother was and still is, eternally, the apple of my eye. When I was just two or three years old, I started growing a deep fascination for her. Her golden spectacles, soft wrinkled skin, the no-teeth cute smile, and the warmth in her eyes, lit up my entire life. I used to sleep in her bed, snugged in between my grandfather and her. Oh, those were the days! What I wouldn't do to get them back.

My pet name is Joyee, essentially in Bengali meaning, victory. However, to do justice, I can also be described as Kangaroo's baby, accompanying my grandma wherever she would go. Whether it's her best friend 'Nomita Mashi's' house or her other friend, 'Baby Pishi', I was quite the devoted granddaughter. But, it was of course, always hard to compete with her devotion towards me. From spoiling me with ice-cream soda, and gold jewellery, to loving me to bits, and not letting my father or grandpa scold me, her love was so effortless and giving towards me, that it can't be described in words. I slowly got introduced to my roots, was pampered rotten, and had a very blessed life, listening to 'Thakumar Jhuli,' (a compilation of Bengali folktales) in the afternoon, recited by her, and I would, till date, do anything to get that same moment back. Wishful thinking, I know!

However, the looming night came, and just like that, her health started to deteriorate; she became skin and bones, until one fine day, she needed support to stand. Full-time nurses were appointed to take care of her, and I think this is the time, I started to put my guard up. How? I knew she was old, and now, with her deteriorating health, I knew she will be with me as long as she can. I somehow eternalised that she is strong-headed and will pull through many more years. You see, when you are young, you often do not foresee what's coming.

However, one fine day, I was taking my EVS tuition, when I heard someone banging at the door. It was my house help telling me how my grandmother is going out of breath. I went running to my drawing room where she used to be sleeping, and there she was. Gasping for her breath, she had her hands raised towards me, asking for help perhaps. I felt my life crashing into pieces. *I* felt breathless too. And then the worst thing possible happened: she left for her heavenly abode.

For me, it was hitting absolute rock bottom.

"Thakuma chole gelo" (Grandma left me) —is what I felt at that moment.

Immediately, my life took a 360-degree turn; the most important person in my life was no more. The pain felt unbearable. I was just sixteen, just got promoted to class 11, and was simply unprepared to deal with the vacuum that followed her passing away. 11th November 2013, I will never forget you! It's been eleven long years.

The Second Gem — My pet dog, Mishti

I was as young as twelve years old, when a very special person entered my life. I call her my daughter, my pet dog, Mishti. It all happened when I was in class 8, and I deeply yearned for a dog. In the past, my family used to boast of being the host of seven gorgeous cats and three dogs, but, deeply saddened by their loss, no one was much eager to get any new pets in the house. Somehow, I managed to convince my grandmother to help me otherwise. With her saved money, I went all the way to Vardhaan Market and got home a 1-month-old spitz, who gave the best ever yawn upon picking her up in the palms of my hands. It was a perfect match. I can never forget that moment. It felt like I just became a new mom. Then, as time passed by, Mishti grew highly affectionate towards me. And so did I, towards her. I loved bathing her, preparing her morning Cerelac, and taking her out for walks. It was blissful.

After all, you don't need much in life when you have the ardent attention of your four-legged friend. Mishti used to follow me everywhere, lick me, wait for me near the door whenever I left the house, and loved getting cuddles from me. It's like I had found my life's purpose. She had biting tendencies, but, I would like to see that as her establishing clear boundaries.

You see, your first dog will always be the most special one. There are no two ways about it. I completed my school, my college, my masters, got my first job, and there she was, always by my side, until 2023, when I lost her. It literally felt like Skyfall!

When a human passes away, you rationalise things faster. You know they had expressed signs of suffering; you know they were in pain, and when they showed signs of deterioration, you could hear what they had to say about their struggles. But when a pet dies, the pain becomes a bit more. Everything feels 5x more than what you would feel in case of your favourite human, because pets have immense pain tolerance, and they cannot speak for themselves. It is only in the absolute end that you realise that your beloved pet is in pain. Sometimes, it can be too late too. So, you somehow hold yourself accountable for what follows with your pet, as you are the one in charge.

After growing older, Mishti soon started showing signs of old age when she became twelve, developing cysts, breathing issues, then recurring eye infections, and a bad loss of appetite. I could feel that the spark that she previously used to have in her eyes is now no more. In fact, she had cataracts in both eyes. Again, signs of old age. I was full of hope and determination, though, much like in my grandmother's time. But again, the same fate followed. Mishti soon had difficulty seeing, walking, eating, and used to be out of breath most of the time. Imagine the pain she must have been in. But, what I loved the most about her was how she never gave up hope and took her medications, maybe because she wanted to obey me or because she wanted to get better, who knows?

The doctor suspected mouth cancer, due to which Mishti was having trouble opening her mouth, leading to appetite loss. I found a ray of hope that an initial diagnosis could be done. The solution was to put her under anaesthesia and check inside her mouth for accurate diagnosis. My intention was for her to get better, and at least live a year or two longer, now that she was fourteen years old. But, sadly, this time, she didn't come back.

I asked myself, 'Did this just happen due to my wrong decision-making?'

Mishti was first injected with an elementary dose of anaesthesia. She tried to protest greatly, but I held her tightly to let the doctor's assistants do what they were doing. Then, when put on the floor for some time, Mishti seemed to have lost balance, but, she still tried to come near me, attracted by my smell, as if asking for help. The doctors observed that she was getting very hostile upon being touched, and they wanted to increase the dosage by using the gas treatment. I, as a pet mom, determined to get a solution and pray for her long lifespan, and in the greed of having her by my side longer, gave consent.

It was then that in 5-minutes time, Mishti was proclaimed dead. Dead, just like that. I couldn't fathom what had just happened. The loss felt personal. I held her body as if she would come back for one last time. But in vain.

This matter is very nascent, just as of 2023. I still haven't healed completely, but, all I know in my conscience is that I had pure intentions only, and I hope that my dog has forgiven me. The series of ifs and buts loom over your head. You never know how the path not taken would be.

Memories

Whatever I have expressed above, is a compilation of my good and bad memories involving two precious souls who have crossed the rainbow bridge. While I wait for the day to get reunited with them, I try to carry their memories with me wherever I go, starting from my grandmom's caresses, warm gestures, and her longing for me to my Mishti's smile, love, and unconditional loyalty.

Will I ever forget them? No, I believe. After all, these were the best moments of my life, the moments of *dolce far niente.*

Today, as I try to don new roles and do the best in my life, their memories feel etched forever in my heart. I would like to call them the two most influential women in my life, shaping another rookie woman's life. If I look back, my grandmom taught me resilience, faith, traditions, and introduced me to society and taught me the walks of womanhood. Mishti, on the other hand, introduced me to the qualities of maternal instinct, patience, understanding non-verbal gestures, and, in general, communicating with animals.

It shall never be forgotten.

Acceptance

After going through the phases of 'complicated grief' and 'emotional paralysis', it's right to believe that the phase of 'acceptance' follows next. And so, with time, the pain begins to soften, not because it disappears, but, because you learn to carry it differently. You realise that acceptance doesn't mean forgetting; it means finding a new way to live with what's been lost. The memories no longer feel like bad baggage, weighing you down, but, rather like golden moments, embedded in the physiology of who you are. Each memory, each lesson, becomes a part of your strength.

You begin to understand that loss, though heartbreaking, can also be a mentor—showing you the mirror, demonstrating the depth of your own resilience and capacity for love. Yes, you have changed, but, perhaps, that change was always meant to happen. And when you look back, you know that the people you've lost will always be with you, not as ghosts of the past, but as guiding lights leading you forward.

With a quiet smile, you walk on—wiser, stronger, and braver. You know your loved ones are never truly gone. They live on in your heart, your actions, and your newly acquired thoughts. And in the quiet moments, when you pause to listen, you can almost hear them cheering you on, proud of how far you've come.

8

To Mammam, My Constant!

Dr. Debasri Mukherjee

I remember, I remember, her toothless smile,
The twinkle in her eyes and the spring in her stride.
I remember, I remember, her stories old and new,
With every morsel of rice and every spoon of stew.
I remember, I remember, the pride in her gait,
When I brought home the marks from my school tests.
I remember, I remember, the warmth of her hug,
Her smell of homemade curry, and her tin tea mug.
I remember, I remember, how she showed me the way,
With her life and her knowledge, Oh! How I miss her every day!

9

The Bridge

Dr. Debosree Ghosh

It was a lovely day, and I had taken a day off from my current workplace to visit my previous workplace and collect some important documents. A wave of nostalgia washed over me, filling mc with happiness. I left my little toddler in the care of my parents, since her father had to rush off to an urgent meeting at his office. I hopped into a cab and made my way to Howrah station. After catching the local train from platform two, I arrived at Hooghly, where I gathered my documents, caught up with old colleagues, and enjoyed a delightful time. I got my work done earlier than expected. On my way back home, I stopped at a local market nearby and picked up two lovely frocks for my daughter as a keepsake from my former workplace. With my tasks completed quicker than anticipated, I returned to Howrah station. Once I arrived at Howrah, I went to the bus station and found a bus heading to my place in Behala. I settled into a ladies' seat, and the bus, which was already half full, waited at the depot.

As I sat there, a woman entered the bus and made her way directly towards me. I can still picture her elegant face; she had a fair complexion, a bright red bindi adorned her forehead and there was red sindoor in her hair. She appeared to be middle-aged and was wearing a beautiful pink saree. She greeted me with a warm smile, and I assumed that she wanted to take the empty seat next to me. However, I couldn't help but wonder why she had chosen to approach me, when there were plenty of other seats available. She came right up to me, smiled, and asked in Bengali if I was headed to Behala. I confirmed that I was. Then, she expressed her belief that the bus would be delayed and suggested that I shouldn't wait for it to start its journey. Her insistence made me feel uneasy, as she was a complete stranger. She urged me to get off the bus, mentioning that she too would take another one. Raising her voice, she also tried to encourage the other passengers to take a different bus on the same route. But, most of them ignored her.

I began to realize that what she had said was indeed true. As I gazed out of the window, I caught sight of a Howrah - Behala mini bus slowly departing from the depot. In an instant, I decided to catch that bus, convinced that it would get me to Behala faster than the one I was currently on. When I turned around, I was taken aback to find that the lady who had urged me to get off the bus had vanished! I assumed that she must have hurried to catch the mini bus as well. I, too, quickly got off and boarded it. I felt really happy with my decision as the bus was speeding up and within thirty minutes, I arrived at my stop in Behala from Howrah station.

Though I never saw that lady again, I silently expressed my gratitude to her. I was eager to return home to my little girl as soon as possible. As I stepped off the bus and walked towards my house, I encountered my uncle, who looked astonished to see me. He asked how I had arrived and then revealed that a major disaster had just occurred. I was surprised and inquired about what had happened. He explained that the bridge over Majherhaat, "The Majherhaat Bridge" had collapsed, injuring many and claiming numerous lives. All the vehicles on the bridge had fallen with it. (The Majherhaat Bridge, constructed over fifty years ago, served as the sole direct link to Behala, South 24 Parganas, and the southern suburbs of Kolkata. As a result, it became the primary route for nearly all vehicles travelling to Behala. I had heard a lot of stories about the bridge from my grandfather and it has been a part of my life since childhood, as we frequently crossed it.)

I couldn't believe my ears! I was overwhelmed with shock, realizing how fortunate I was to have taken that mini bus. Otherwise, I could have been stuck in traffic for hours or, worse, been on the bridge during the collapse. My uncle shared my shock and relief, thanking the divine and offering a prayer. My thoughts drifted back to the lady; her image remained etched in my memory. I felt as if she had been sent by a higher power to guide me to safety. The thought of what could have happened if she hadn't approached me that day sent shivers down my spine. I was terrified at the idea of leaving my little one at home, while narrowly escaping a life-threatening situation. It took me quite a few years to come to terms with that day, the 4th of September, 2018. The date, the woman, the event, and my final trip across the historic bridge, along with my close call with disaster, are all memories that will remain etched in my mind for eternity.

It took several years to reconstruct the bridge, and during that time, an alternative route was necessary to access Behala. The bridge's collapse resulted in the tragic loss of several lives, leaving many others with severe injuries, some even facing lifelong paralysis and trauma. That day, a remarkable woman became my saviour—an angel in disguise—who assisted a mother in reuniting with her young child safely and on time. This experience has deepened my belief that God has a unique plan for each one of us, guiding our lives along a predetermined path.

ÞÞÞ

10

My 'Uncle', Subhasji

Santanu Ghosal

The man I knew as 'Uncle' for forty years, has decided to move on. I met him in 1981-82 as a year 9 student, when common friends took me across to play 'galli' cricket (& lagori & badminton), on this mysteriously empty plot of land adjacent to Uncle's house. Over the course of the next ten years, he became my father-in-law and then a friend. I lost a friend today. Covid, managed to take him away from us. Never, ever, did we think that the man we lovingly called the 'Steel Man', would succumb so quickly.

Although his passing broke our collective hearts, I set out to write this piece as a celebration of the life of this extraordinarily happy human being. Yes, above all else, he personified the essence of humanity. At first glance, especially in his younger days, he seemed quite intimidating. His finely chiselled features, magnificent physique and enormous strength earned him the 'Steel Man' sobriquet. The 'tough' image, however, melted away dramatically as soon as he broke into his trademark grin, engulfing you in its warmth. This 'Steel' part of his personality probably had something to do with the fact that he spent all his working life at Tata Steel (erstwhile TISCO), living and breathing the ethos of the Tatas and 'steel' making.

Subhas Madhavrao Apte was the lynch pin of the extended Apte family. His elder brother, Shri Chandrakant Apte (Anna), would be completely lost without Subhasji, while the latter worshipped Anna and his amazing musical talent. For his three nieces, 'Kaka' could manage anything at any time of the day. Subhasji's childhood friends knew that they could always depend upon him to get them out of trouble. Even money, or the lack of it, never fazed him.

Gifted with an amazing voice and an even more fantastic memory, he never got to train as a classical vocalist – at least not formally. However, the hours he spent listening to and accompanying Anna, turned him into an encyclopedia of Hindustani classical music and its masterful (and often colourful) practitioners. His love of music encompassed the entire spectrum, from Hindustani classical to Hindi film music, Bengali – Rabindrasangeet, Nazrul geeti and *adhunik*, and even extended to the odd English tracks! Leo Sayer's rendition of "I love you more than I can say..." never failed to move him.

The man who made everyone smile with his unique phrases – "E babu jara ***fat-ne-se*** samosa le aana", "jara ***kamar jhuka ke jharu lagayo, tum to Tisco ke rejayon jaise jharu laga rahe ho***!" He always loved a good haggle – whether it be the rickshawalla, the jalebi maker ("***garam tel mein hi talna***!"), the Sakchi (Jamshedpur), or Laxmi Road (Pune) clothes retailers, even extending to the bigger eating joints in the malls! His love of eating and treating was legendary. Absolute Barbeques, Bar-b-q Nation (till it fell out of favour!), Mainland China, et al were his regular haunts, especially and often in the company of his enthusiastic grandchildren. The following conversation ensued every time I visited him –

"Santanu boss **Independence** (the local microbrewery) ***chalte hain***?"

"***Par Uncle aap toh piyenge nahin***?"

"***Toh kya hua tum ko German style 'wit beer' pilana hai***!"

He loved making and serving the most delectable omelettes and his masala chai was to die for! The local *breadwala*, the *andewala*, the *panwalla* and the pharmacist were all examples of his natural ability to bond with people, irrespective of their social standing!

While he stood like a rock for his family and friends, his anchor was his 'Vyjayantimala', his wife and partner of fifty-five years, Madhura. Through thick and thin, the tough times and the good times, this amazing partnership nurtured an extended family that I feel privileged to be part of. His obvious pride in the achievements of his children and their families and his ability to 'entertain' his grandchildren endeared him to all.

We will all miss our friend, but, his parting gift to us - this vast album of memories filled with music, laughter and fun

- will make us smile every time we remember him.

♡♡♡

Author Biography

11

Dr. Sukanya Bhattacharya

Dr. Sukanya Bhattacharya is an Associate Professor in the Department of Botany, Vidyasagar College, Kolkata. Dr. Bhattacharya has a brilliant academic profile with high

First class in both B.Sc and M.Sc exams of Calcutta University. She had been a National Scholar and had the distinction of being a Direct Fellow CSIR, New Delhi. She obtained her Ph.D from Jadavpur University and since then had been a member of several learned bodies in India such as Life member Indian Science Congress Association, Life member Eastern India Horticulture and Biotechnology Centre. She has delivered several lectures at a number of symposia, seminars and conferences in India. She has several original research papers published in National and International journals of repute.In addition to academics, Dr. Bhattacharya is also deeply interested in art, literature and music.

12

Deyasini Roy

Deyasini Roy, a post graduate in Sociology from St Xavier's College, Kolkata, and currently an aspirant of government examinations, holds a keen interest in writing. She also carries a passion for singing and cooking. She firmly believes in the saying that "The pen is mightier than the sword", as words supremely heal one's internal injuries as well as crucifies the wrongs of the society at large, which cannot be erased or reversed.

13

Monoswita Biswas

I am Monoswita Biswas. I have completed my M.A in English from the University of Calcutta. I follow my dreams and in my leisure time I enjoy writing. I love reading novels, especially those that belong to the Victorian period. Novelists like George Eliot, Thomas

Hardy, and Charles Dickens are my favourites. As far as poetry is concerned, all the English Romantic poets are my favourite.

14

Dr. Debasri Mukherjee

I was born and grew up in a joint family in Kolkata, West Bengal, India. At that time everyone knew it as Calcutta.My schooling was at Loreto Convent. I went on to do my Bachelors and Masters in Human Physiology from the University of Calcutta. Then I did my Ph.D in Cardiovascular Physiology also from the Dept. of Physiology, University of Calcutta, under the supervision of Prof Debasish Bandyopadhyay.I did my post-doctoral research in immune-cell biology and proteomics from the National Centre for Cell Science of the Dept. of Biotechnology, GOI, in Pune, Maharashtra, India. Then I joined Cactus Communications Pvt Ltd as a Scientific Writer.I am passionate about writing and have dabbled in multiple genres of fiction writing, from ghost stories to children's tales. Other than that, I enjoy swimming, traveling, and reading story books.My family comprises my parents, my aunt and uncle, my mother-in-law, my husband, and our black Labrador named Nemo (from Jules Verne's Captain Nemo. Not the fish).

15

Sanchita Chakraborty

Sanchita Chakraborty is a teacher at K. E. Carmel School, Suri. She holds a Master's degree in English and Culture Studies from The University of Burdwan. Passionate about exploring life through words, Sanchita inspires all to appreciate the shades of language and literature.

16

Shreya Ghose

Shreya Ghose is a corporate professional with a rich background in media, communications, and creative arts. Born and raised in Kolkata, she graduated in Mass Communication & Videography (Hons) from St. Xavier's College, Kolkata before moving to Mumbai to pursue a

Master's degree in Media & Advertising, from KC College, Mumbai University. Shreya's career began in public relations with Dentsu Perfect Relations, where she handled high-profile FMCG, technology, automobile, and pharmaceutical brands. She later shifted to celebrity PR, working with Raindrop, and collaborating with prominent Bollywood personalities before transitioning to content marketing, where she honed her expertise in writing, content strategy, SEO, and social media.Currently, Shreya works as a Corporate Communications professional for a multinational company, managing branding for three deep-tech brands based in Kolkata. Beyond her corporate role, Shreya is also a certified makeup artist from Lakme Academy, reflecting her passion for creativity and the arts. An animal lover at heart, Shreya shares a deep bond for furry friends. When not working, she enjoys cooking, driving, swimming, and indulging in her love for documentaries, movies, and makeup.Shreya's diverse skills, passion for learning, and creative pursuits make her a dynamic storyteller and communicator.

17

Dr. Debosree Ghosh

Dr. Debosree Ghosh is an Assistant Professor in the Department of Physiology, Government General Degree College, Kharagpur II, West Bengal, India. Dr. Ghosh has been awarded Gold Medal by the University of Calcutta for holding 1st rank in M.Sc. in Human Physiology and received DST INSPIRE Fellowship in 2011 from the Ministry of Science, India, to pursue her Ph.D. in Physiology from the University of Calcutta. She has been awarded the Dr. D.N. Mullick Memorial Prize of the Physiological Society of India. She received a travel grant from the University of Calcutta for presenting her research work at the South Asian Association of Physiologists Conference, held in Colombo, Srilanka. She has been awarded a certificate of merit for the XXVI Training Programme on Science Communication and Media Practice held under the aegis of the Indian Science News Association. She has published more than 90 articles in peer-reviewed national and international journals. She has authored several book chapters in books published by national and international publishers. She has published more than 43 popular science articles in several newsletters. She has authored her first short story "An Unusual Winter Tale" in the anthology 'Winter Musings' published by Rhythmic Publishers. She is on the editorial board and serves as a reviewer in several national and international journals. She has delivered lectures at several national and international conferences in India and abroad.

18

Santanu Ghosal

Santanu Ghoshal is a Bengali hailing from Bihar/ Jharkhand. He grew up in Jamshedpur. He loves reading and is now responding to a strong urge to transfer his thoughts and experiences onto paper. He has lived and worked across different parts

of India and is currently residing
in Australia. He loves playing sports, especially badminton and cricket, and reading about and travelling to places of historical interest.

www.ingramcontent.com/pod-product-compliance
Lightning Source LLC
LaVergne TN
LVHW090132160826
845673LV00017B/2437

* 9 7 9 8 8 9 6 7 3 6 7 2 1 *